Bible Angels & Demons

Bible Angels & Demons

by Rick Osborne & Ed Strauss

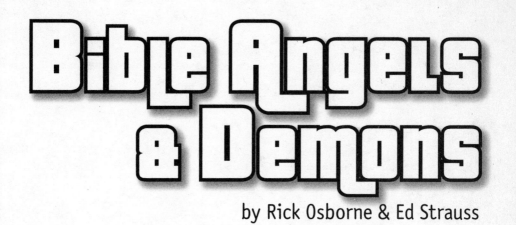

zonderkidz

ZONDERVAN.com/
AUTHORTRACKER
follow your favorite authors

The children's group of Zondervan

www.zonderkidz.com

Bible Angels & Demons
Copyright ® 2004 by Lightwave Publishing
Illustrations Copyright © 2004 by Zondervan

Requests for information should be addressed to:
Grand Rapids, Michigan 49530

Library of Congress Cataloging-in-Publication Data

Osborne, Rick.
  Bible angels and demons / by Rick Osborne.– 1st ed.
    p. cm.
  ISBN-13: 978-0-310-70775-2
  ISBN-10: 0-310-70775-7 (pbk.)

  1. Angels–Biblical teaching–Juvenile literature. 2.   Demonology–Biblical teaching–
Juvenile literature. [1. Angels. 2. Demonology. 3. Bible stories. 4. Christian life.] I. Title.
  BS680.A48O83 2004
  235'.2-dc22   2003026122

Editor: Gwen Ellis
Cover Direction & Design: Merit Alderink
Interior Art Direction: Michelle Lenger
Cover Illustration: Erwin Haya
Interior Illustrations: Anthony Carpenter

Printed in United States of America
08 09 10 • 9 8

news Flash!

We are not alone in this universe. Don't panic. We're not
talking about being invaded by aliens. We're not talking
about aliens from other planets zipping around the galaxy in
flying saucers. We're talking about powerful beings whom
God created. They are not human and do not live on earth.
These fantastic beings don't live up in the stars, either. And
they don't live on other planets. They live in another dimension—the dimension of the spiritual.

That spiritual dimension or supernatural realm is the real
world. The water-covered rock we walk on and call Earth
is just a shadow and copy of that spiritual world. Even our
bodies are just houses for our spirit—the eternal part of us
that fits in that other dimension. One day we won't need our
physical bodies any longer and we will live forever with God
in his fantastic spiritual realm.

In that world lives a Being so awesome, so super-intelligent,
and so powerful that he is beyond our comprehension.
We're talking about God, of course. He is a spiritual being
and he lives in the spiritual dimension. In fact, he created
this people-populated planet and the physical universe from
the spiritual dimension.

God also created all kinds of amazing beings that now populate the spiritual dimension. Some of them, like the cherubim, have unimaginable power and appear to act as God's ceremonial bodyguards and his private worship team. Others called just plain "angels" exist to serve mankind. Now understand this: angels are not drifting around like some kind of limp feather dusters. They are very powerful creatures with blazing eyes and superhuman intelligence that is sometimes downright scary!

The spiritual realm is not only full of amazing beings, but it's also full of mind-blowing things and places. This spiritual dimension is not confined to one little planet such as the world we know—Planet Earth. The spiritual world has a bright side and a dark side. The bright side has lands and scenery like nothing you've ever seen—like nothing you could even imagine. The dark side includes places you would not want to go to, such as the lake of burning sulfur—Hell. And speaking of hell, the dark side of the spirit world is also populated by horrible beings—the Devil and his demons (angels that were evicted from God's presence).

In *Bible Angels & Demons*, we plan to take a look at what the Bible says about the whole amazing spiritual realm and the mind-boggling beings that populate it.

the SPIRituAL REALm

SPIRITUAL MATTER

"Things" in Heaven

Some people think there are no dimensional objects in the spiritual world just because what exist are not physical objects. People have this picture of heaven as a place with spirits floating around in the mist with clouds and fog banks rolling around them. Huh? That's heaven? I don't thiiiink so. If there are no real things in heaven, what are angels' clothes made of? What about the chariots they cruise in? And did you know Jesus is going to return to earth riding a horse? Even though things in the spiritual dimension are not the physical things we know, they are still real. They are real and they are solid—though not to human eyes and hands. We were created to see and touch and experience physical matter. We were not built for the spiritual dimension. But to spiritual beings, spiritual objects in that other dimension are very real. Colossians 1:16 says, "For by him [God] all things were created: things in heaven and on earth."

What's Up There?

There are hints in the Bible about what heaven is like. If you really want to get a big download of information, read the last two chapters of Revelation. Streets of gold! A river of life and the Tree of Life! Mind you, we don't know if some of these descriptions are literal (like what you read is exactly what you get) or whether they're symbolic—the writer is trying to describe things that we don't have words to describe.

These two chapters in Revelation tell us what heaven will be like after Jesus comes back to earth. When we read it, we can see that God was trying to give us a glimpse of a place that's beyond phenomenal. We can also tell that heaven is not one big huge cloud bank like a bad day at the wharf in Seattle or Vancouver. Heaven is not just fog and smoke. It is a real place.

When Jesus was saying good-bye to his disciples, he told them, "In my Father's house are many rooms ... I am going there to prepare a place for you" (John 14:2). Cool! So just what kind of place is he preparing for us? A lot better than your present bedroom, that's for sure! First Corinthians 2:9 says, "No eye has seen, no ear has heard, no mind has conceived what God has prepared for those who love him." We can't even make it up because it is way better than anything we can imagine. The Bible gives us glimpses of what heaven is like now. Let's take a look.

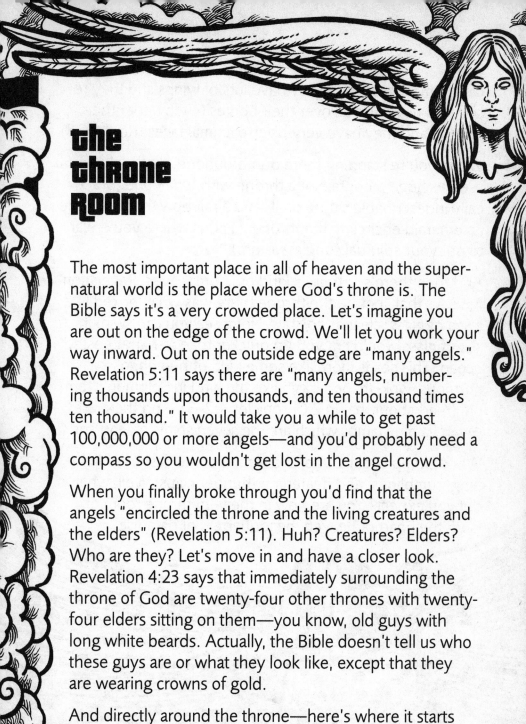

the throne room

The most important place in all of heaven and the supernatural world is the place where God's throne is. The Bible says it's a very crowded place. Let's imagine you are out on the edge of the crowd. We'll let you work your way inward. Out on the outside edge are "many angels." Revelation 5:11 says there are "many angels, numbering thousands upon thousands, and ten thousand times ten thousand." It would take you a while to get past 100,000,000 or more angels—and you'd probably need a compass so you wouldn't get lost in the angel crowd.

When you finally broke through you'd find that the angels "encircled the throne and the living creatures and the elders" (Revelation 5:11). Huh? Creatures? Elders? Who are they? Let's move in and have a closer look. Revelation 4:23 says that immediately surrounding the throne of God are twenty-four other thrones with twenty-four elders sitting on them—you know, old guys with long white beards. Actually, the Bible doesn't tell us who these guys are or what they look like, except that they are wearing crowns of gold.

And directly around the throne—here's where it starts getting really wild—are these four ... well ... all you can call them is creatures. They have lots of wings and they're covered with eyes all over their bodies (even under their wings!) and they have very bizarre animal faces (Rev. 4:6-8).

When you're standing there dumbfounded, that's when you see this huge mountain of a throne with "someone" practically indescribable sitting on it, and a rainbow that looks like an emerald encircling the throne. (This is where you'd want to put your spiritual sunglasses on.)

And then there's ... there's kind of ... um ... well, Revelation 4:6 says that "before the throne there was what looked like a sea of glass, clear as crystal." Not a sea you can swim in. A sea of glass would cut you up quicker than a shark-infested ocean. This sea is more like some kind of humongo-normous, wok-shaped basin like the kind in Solomon's temple (read about that in 2 Chronicles 4:2–3). And there are seven flaming lamps which are the seven spirits of God and ...

Whoa! Jump back! Out of the throne come flashes of lightning, rumblings, and deafening thunder claps. Well, what did you expect? You are now in the very throne room of God, the heart of heaven, headquarters of paradise.

WHAT FOUR PROPHETS SAW

In the Bible, there were four prophets who had visions of God sitting on his throne. Here's what they saw:

Isaiah: The prophet Isaiah said, "I saw the Lord seated on a throne, high and exalted ... Above him were seraphs, each with six wings" (Isaiah 6:1–2).

Ezekiel: One day Ezekiel saw a cloud with flashing lightning, fire, and brilliant light. The center of the fire looked like glowing metal. Then he saw the figure of a man—God, that is—sitting on a throne of deep blue sapphire. From his waist up God looked like glowing metal full of fire! From the waist down he looked like fire, and brilliant light surrounded him. He was glowing like a rainbow (Ezekiel 1:4, 26–28).

Daniel: Daniel saw God on his throne too. He said, "the Ancient of Days took his seat. His clothing was as white as snow; the hair of his head was white like wool. His throne was flaming with fire, and its wheels were all ablaze. A river of fire was flowing, coming out from before him" (Daniel 7:9–10).

John: When the apostle John visited heaven he saw "a throne in heaven ... and the one who sat there had the

appearance of jasper and carnelian. A rainbow, resembling an emerald, encircled the throne" (Revelation 4:2–3).

In God's Presence

God told Moses, "You cannot see my face, for no one may see me and live" (Exodus 33:20). Some people have seen God in a vision and they didn't die. But if God broke through from the other dimension and appeared in person before you, you'd fall over dead. The last thing you'd see before you hit the floor would be someone looking like glowing, white-hot metal mixed with fire and the gemstones of jasper and carnelian. There would be a rainbow glowing around him.

Isaiah 45:15 says, "Truly you are a God who hides himself." God doesn't hide himself because he wants to be hidden. He hides himself because our physical senses are set up to handle physical experiences. If we were to experience the brightness of God's spiritual glory with our physical senses, we couldn't take it. The good news is that when we leave this life we'll be transformed and we'll be able to go right into God's presence.

Peek At My Back

The only way people could see God and not die was if (a) he disguised himself in a normal human body or a cloud, (b) they saw him in a vision, or (c) they went to heaven (in their spirits) and saw him there. Moses often saw the pillar of cloud that represented God to his people, but one day Moses wanted to see what God really looked like. So he said, "Now show me your glory." God replied, "You cannot see my face, for no one may see me and live." ("Well, when you put it that way ... ") But God did the next best thing. He plopped Moses into a crevice in the cliff and covered him with his hand until he passed by. Then he removed his hand and—WHOA!—Moses saw God's back and even that probably half-blinded him (Exodus 33:18–23).

Glowing Like a Light Bulb

Ever had one of those toys where you hold it near light and it absorbs light, then you turn off the light and it keeps on glowing? Moses had an experience like that, only cooler. A zillion times cooler. He spent forty days up on the mountain talking with God and when he came back down his face was glowing so much people were afraid to go near him. He had to cover his face (Exodus 34:29–35).

You Can't Go In. *God's* In There

If God came to your church in his full glory, you would not be able to go through the front door. His presence would be so powerful you'd be knocked flat on the doorsill. Well, after Moses set up the tabernacle, the Bible says he "could not enter the Tent of Meeting because the cloud had settled upon it, and the glory of the Lord filled the tabernacle" (Exodus 40:35). Another time when Solomon dedicated the temple to God, the priests could not enter it because God's glory filled it (2 Chronicles 7:1–2). Nothing to fool around with, guys.

God's "Hot Wheels"

Hey, did you get a clue earlier when you read that Daniel had said God's throne had "blazing wheels"? So what's God's throne doing with "hot wheels"? We don't know. When Ezekiel had a vision of God on his throne, he also described wheels. He said they were sparkling like chrysolite (a greenyellow gem) and each one appeared to be like a wheel intersecting a wheel. Got that figured out? No? Well, welcome to the club. Many artists have scratched their heads trying to draw what Ezekiel described. But here's something else. Not only are these wheels flaming or sparkling, and intersecting each other, they're also full of eyeballs (read it for yourself in Ezekiel 1:16–18).

At His Right Hand

We know that God's throne is awesome, but guess what? Jesus said, "I overcame and sat down with my Father on his throne" (Revelation 3:21). When Jesus went up to heaven, he sat down at the right hand of God (Mark 16:19). Here's one for you to figure out. The Bible teaches us that God is three in one; God the Father, God the Son, and God the Holy Spirit. So if John saw God the Father sitting on the throne and Jesus the Son is seated at God's right hand, where's the Holy Spirit? Figured it out yet? He's here on earth working in the Church, through Christians—through us—through our hearts and lives.

Where Is God? Where *Isn't* He?

Just when we finish telling you that God is seated on a throne in heaven, now we gotta tell you that he's not just there, he's everywhere! There's a big word called omni-present that describes God's ability to be everywhere at the same time. That's what "omnipresent" means—"being everywhere at once."

When King Solomon was building a temple for God, he admitted, "Who is able to build a temple for him, since the heavens, even the highest heavens, cannot contain him?" (2 Chronicles 2:6). "Big" doesn't even begin to describe God! David said that you can't hide from God (Psalm 139:7–12). No matter where you go, he's there.

But how can God be sitting on his throne and still be everywhere at the same time? It's a little hard to understand (truthfully, it's impossible to understand). Just remember, God invented everything. He invented the universe. He invented time and space. So even though we are limited by these laws and can only be in one place in one minute, God is not limited. He's in everything he created, he's outside everything he created, and he's also way beyond everything he created. Chew on that a while.

God's Bio in Brief

We know God is omniscient (that means all-knowing). In other words, he knows everything about everything! God is also omnipotent—which means all-powerful. Nothing is more powerful than he is. Nothing is too hard for him! God is also eternal, which means he has no beginning and no end. He always has been and always will be. God is holy, perfect, and unchanging. Wow! Awesome God! But wait—there's more. The apostle John described the very best thing about God: "God is love" (1 John 4:16). It's pretty great to have a God that awesome who also loves you and calls you his child.

get deeper

There's a scripture that makes it clear God has rolled out the red carpet for all of us who have accepted Jesus and live for him. "You have come to Mount Zion, to the heavenly Jerusalem, the city of the living God. You have come to thousands upon thousands of angels in joyful assembly, to the church of the firstborn, whose names are written in heaven. You have come to God, the judge of all men, to the spirits of righteous men made perfect, to Jesus the mediator" (Hebrews 12:22–24). You see, we have our invitation to heaven and we're expected to show up. When we get there, we'll cross dimensions to that supernatural world. There we'll live in heaven, see God's throne, and be with him forever. Now that's something to look forward to!

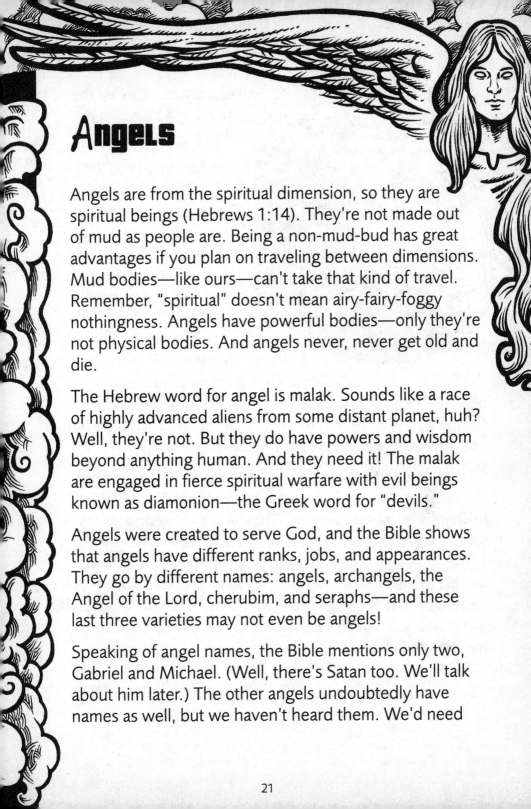

Angels

Angels are from the spiritual dimension, so they are spiritual beings (Hebrews 1:14). They're not made out of mud as people are. Being a non-mud-bud has great advantages if you plan on traveling between dimensions. Mud bodies—like ours—can't take that kind of travel. Remember, "spiritual" doesn't mean airy-fairy-foggy nothingness. Angels have powerful bodies—only they're not physical bodies. And angels never, never get old and die.

The Hebrew word for angel is malak. Sounds like a race of highly advanced aliens from some distant planet, huh? Well, they're not. But they do have powers and wisdom beyond anything human. And they need it! The malak are engaged in fierce spiritual warfare with evil beings known as diamonion—the Greek word for "devils."

Angels were created to serve God, and the Bible shows that angels have different ranks, jobs, and appearances. They go by different names: angels, archangels, the Angel of the Lord, cherubim, and seraphs—and these last three varieties may not even be angels!

Speaking of angel names, the Bible mentions only two, Gabriel and Michael. (Well, there's Satan too. We'll talk about him later.) The other angels undoubtedly have names as well, but we haven't heard them. We'd need

quite a big book to list the names of a hundred million angels.

What do angels look like? When they appear to humans, they look like people—only they're so full of supernatural power, they glow with light. One angel is described this way: "His appearance was like lightning" (Matthew 28:3) and two angels at the tomb of Jesus are described as being dressed in "clothes that gleamed like lightning" (Luke 24:4). No, these guys didn't stick their fingers in electrical outlets. They just glow naturally.

So they are powerful and they show up looking very scary, but what do they do? The list is pretty long. One of their main jobs is to help humans. They are "ministering spirits sent to serve those who will inherit salvation" (Hebrews 1:14). That's us! They also carry messages, blind entire cities, kill thousands of soldiers, slay false prophets, battle demons, and the list goes on. You know, they do angel stuff. So let's look at what the Bible says about these fascinating messengers of God.

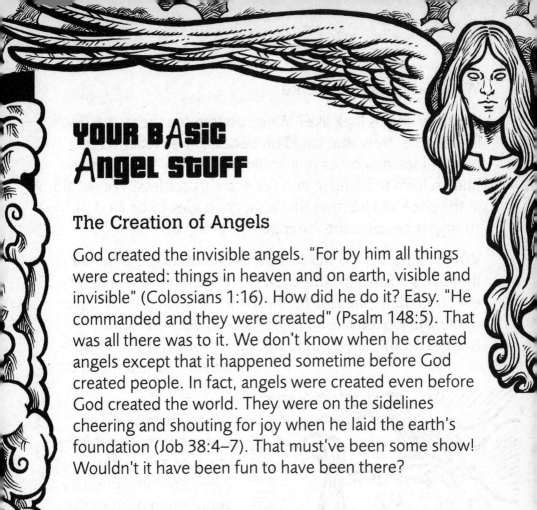

YOUR BASIC Angel STUFF

The Creation of Angels

God created the invisible angels. "For by him all things were created: things in heaven and on earth, visible and invisible" (Colossians 1:16). How did he do it? Easy. "He commanded and they were created" (Psalm 148:5). That was all there was to it. We don't know when he created angels except that it happened sometime before God created people. In fact, angels were created even before God created the world. They were on the sidelines cheering and shouting for joy when he laid the earth's foundation (Job 38:4–7). That must've been some show! Wouldn't it have been fun to have been there?

How Many Angels?

No one knows how many angels there are, but Daniel 7:10 says thousands upon thousands and ten thousand times ten thousand angels stand before God's throne. When John made his cross-dimension trip to heaven, he saw the same number of angels around God's throne (Revelation 5:11). That's like ... more than 100 million angels!

What Angels Look Like

What do angels look like? When people see them, they look like people. Now that could be because they really have human-looking bodies or it could be because they take on human form to blend in and not scare us spitless. We're told in the book of Hebrews that it's a good idea to be kind to strangers because the "stranger" just might be an angel.

When Samson's mother met the Angel of the Lord before there was a Samson, she knew there was something different about him. She told her husband, "A man of God came to me. He looked like an angel of God, very awesome" (Judges 13:6). She thought he was a prophet, but she wondered if he just might be an angel.

When you see angels without their secret identity gear and ready to rip, there's nothing ordinary about them. Picture the angel Daniel saw: "His body was like chrysolite, his face like lightning, his eyes like flaming torches, his arms and legs like the gleam of burnished bronze, and his voice like the sound of a multitude" (Daniel 10:6). The angel Daniel saw was a powerful, important angel. Maybe this angel was just so great and glorious that he couldn't stuff it all into human skin and pass himself off as a normal person. Maybe there are plain, regular angels, and we already know there are other magnificent glowing ones that look like lightning bolts in lightning clothes. Whatever they look like, all angels are cool and powerful.

Angel Eyes

If someone says a girl has "angel eyes," she smiles and sweetly says, "Ah, thank you for the compliment." But here's the truth. Angels' eyeballs glow with light like something out of a scary sci-fi movie. The angel that Daniel saw had "eyes as lamps of fire" (Daniel 10:6 KJV). No wonder people were scared silly and angels had to always tell them, "Don't be afraid." If you were to see an angel with white-hot glowing eyes, bet you'd stay up all night with the hall light on. Hey, but if it helps, it's great to know they're on our side.

Super-Smart? Oh Yeah!

Angels have superhuman intelligence. If some kid in your class were really an angel (not likely), he'd be scoring A$^+$ on every test. God is showing his angels new stuff all the time and they're getting smarter and smarter (Ephesians 3:10).

Angels don't need calculators to figure out complex math equations. Angels are particularly good at figuring out the difference between good and evil (2 Samuel 14:17). But in spite of all that, angels don't know everything. For example, they don't know the day or hour Jesus is coming back to earth (Matthew 24:36). Only God knows.

Do Angels Eat?

Remember what the Israelites ate in the desert for forty years? Psalm 78:24-25 says, "He [God] rained down manna ... he gave them the grain of heaven. Men ate the bread of angels." It sure sounds like angels eat. But grain of heaven? What? Are there like wheat fields inside the heavenly city? Well, we don't know whether angels really have their own food to eat, or even if they need to eat, but we do know they can eat if they choose.

When the Lord and two angels visited Abraham at lunchtime one day, Abraham prepared a meal of tenderloin roast beef, fresh-baked matzo bread, curds, and milk. Then he stood there and watched them chow down. They probably even licked their fingers. (People didn't use spoons and forks back then.) And this wasn't a one-time thing. About seven hours later those same two angels were ready for another round. They helped themselves to a big dinner, thank you very much! (Genesis 18:1–18; 19:1–3).

One time Elijah was mighty discouraged. He lay beneath a broom tree (not a broom some kid had stuck in the sand, but a real tree) and moaned that he wanted to die. After Elijah whined, he fell asleep. He slept until an angel woke him and gave him water and freshly-baked bread. Mmm-mmmm! Smells good! Elijah ate and drank and zonked right out again. The angel woke him up again and told him to go for seconds, so he did. "And now I am truly stuffed!" That meal gave Elijah strength for a forty-day hike (1 Kings 19:1–8). Two meals that keep you going for forty days? Think of the money your parents could save on groceries if they had that recipe. "No thanks, Mom. I ate last month."

Hmmm, Abraham cooked for angels and they were hungry again right away. Angels cooked for Elijah and he wasn't hungry again for forty days. So whom would you want to cook for you—Abraham or angels?

Baby Angels?

There is no record in the Bible of baby angels or little kid angels or angels growing up. Jesus said that angels never get married (Luke 20:34–36) so we can assume that they don't have babies. That means God created all angels as originals.

Do you think he created them one at a time or all at once? If it was all at once, that would have been some sight! One minute no angels, the next minute 100 million of them were standing around wondering what to do next.

get smarter

As we've seen, even though angels are awesome, incredible beings, God made them so that they can still learn and grow. First Peter 1:12 says that a topic they're excited to learn about is God's salvation plan for humankind and what he's doing on earth through his Son, Jesus. Wow! If salvation is so cool and exciting that angels want to learn more about it, then shouldn't we be even more excited to learn all we can?

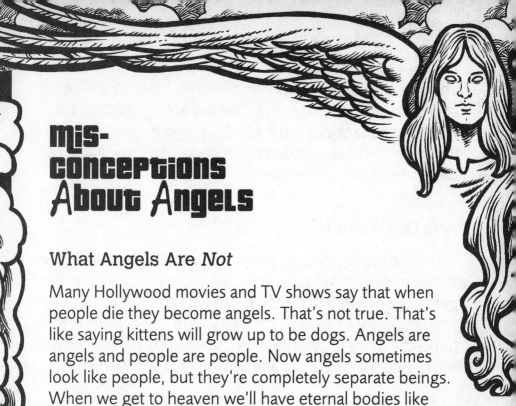

mis-conceptions About Angels

What Angels Are *Not*

Many Hollywood movies and TV shows say that when people die they become angels. That's not true. That's like saying kittens will grow up to be dogs. Angels are angels and people are people. Now angels sometimes look like people, but they're completely separate beings. When we get to heaven we'll have eternal bodies like angels (1 Corinthians 6:3; 15:42–44), but will we ever become angels? Nope! Never.

Do Angels Have Wings?

Angels can fly. We know that for sure. But we do not know if they have wings. They are spiritual beings and spiritual beings don't have to bother with silly things like the law of gravity. That means angels do not need wings. That's why when Gideon, Manoah (Samson's father), and others saw angels they thought the angels were people (Judges 6:11–22; 13:6–21; Hebrews 13:2). If Gideon had seen angels with big old white wings, he for sure would have thought, "Hmmm. Now there's something strange about this guy. What is it?"

The only heavenly beings that definitely have wings are cherubim and seraphs—and they have four and even six wings each (Ezekiel 1:11; Isaiah 6:2). Some people think that they're types of angels, but the Bible doesn't say. It just calls them cherubim and seraphs.

Any Girl Angels?

There are many paintings of girl angels, and in many movies angels appear as women—with wings, no less. So, are there girl angels? Only in the movies. Angels are neither male nor female. All we can say is that every time an angel appeared to people in the Bible, the angel looked like a man. The Bible never says that there are angels who look like women.

Do Angels Have Halos?

Nope. Next question. Okay, let's explain this one. Angels do glow with light. We've already read about the angel light shows. When "an angel of the Lord appeared to them [the shepherds], and the glory of the Lord shone around them, and they were terrified" (Luke 2:9). In Acts 12:7, "an angel of the Lord appeared and a light shone in the cell." Because in these stories angels' faces sometimes glowed with brilliant light, it became common for painters to show angels with a glow over their head—a halo. But no, there is no glowing Frisbee or ring floating above angels' heads.

Do Angels Play Harps?

Angels might play harps, but the Bible doesn't mention them doing it. They might also play Ping-Pong or football, but the Bible doesn't mention them doing those things either. Seriously now, the Bible tells about a time when angels and all the rest of the heavenly crowd were standing around the throne of God and there was a sound like the music of harps. (Not harps, but like harps.) It was more like "a loud peal of thunder" (Revelation 14:2). Wow! That makes you wonder what kind of amplifiers they had!

get cooler

Hebrews 13:2 says, "Do not forget to entertain strangers, for by so doing some people have entertained angels without knowing it." Now, in case you hadn't guessed, "entertainment" does not mean showing them a video or even juggling apples. Entertainment here means showing them hospitality. Today, in order to stay safe, we need to be careful how we relate to some strangers. We just can't let everyone into our homes. But even though we are careful, we should always be open to helping others.

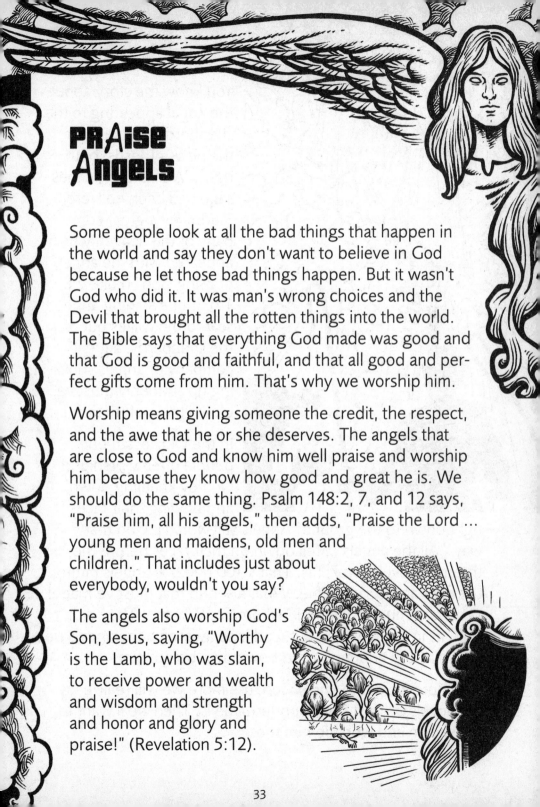

PRAISE Angels

Some people look at all the bad things that happen in the world and say they don't want to believe in God because he let those bad things happen. But it wasn't God who did it. It was man's wrong choices and the Devil that brought all the rotten things into the world. The Bible says that everything God made was good and that God is good and faithful, and that all good and perfect gifts come from him. That's why we worship him.

Worship means giving someone the credit, the respect, and the awe that he or she deserves. The angels that are close to God and know him well praise and worship him because they know how good and great he is. We should do the same thing. Psalm 148:2, 7, and 12 says, "Praise him, all his angels," then adds, "Praise the Lord ... young men and maidens, old men and children." That includes just about everybody, wouldn't you say?

The angels also worship God's Son, Jesus, saying, "Worthy is the Lamb, who was slain, to receive power and wealth and wisdom and strength and honor and glory and praise!" (Revelation 5:12).

You know the story about the angel appearing to the shepherds to give them the news of Jesus' birth, right? Well, after the message had been delivered, "suddenly a great company of the heavenly host appeared with the angel, praising God" (Luke 2:8–14). If one shining angel scared the willies out of the shepherds, a great company of angels showing up suddenly must've blown them off their feet.

In the Old Testament people often worshiped God by kneeling down and bowing their faces right down to the ground. Angels still worship God that way. "All the angels ... fell down on their faces before the throne" (Revelation 7:11). That's 100,000,000 angels hitting the floor at the same time. What a sound that must've made! Whump! Thump! Thump! Fwhummp! Whump! They didn't "fall" as in tumble over, but God is so awesome the angels do love him and adore him and bow down before him.

The more we get to know God, the more we will realize, as the angels do, just how wonderful he is. Then we'll want to praise him and worship him too.

Angelic messengers

Messengers and Mailmen

Angels often appeared to bring messages to people. In fact, the Hebrew word for "angel" (malak) means "messenger." Same with the Greek word for "angel" (aggelos). It means "messenger" too. God often spoke messages directly to his people, but sometimes he sent messages with angels. The prophet Daniel received so many messages from angels that it was a sure thing they had his zip code memorized.

Angels Doing Birth Announcements

Today when a woman is pregnant, the doctor confirms it. But can you imagine a doctor telling someone the news even before the baby is conceived? One time in Israel the Angel of the Lord showed up about a year before the baby was born to tell Manoah and his wife they'd have a baby. "Oh yeah, and your kid will be super-special. He'll start delivering Israel from the Philistines." Sure enough, the woman gave birth to a boy and they named him Samson (Judges 13).

The most famous messenger angel, Gabriel, also surprised several people with birth announcements. Once he dropped in at the temple in Jerusalem when Zacharias was burning incense to God. Gabriel must have been "powered on" and glowing because Zechariah was gripped with fear. Gabriel said, "Do not be afraid," then told him that his wife was going to have a baby (Luke 1:8–20). Three months later Gabriel was back again, this time in Galilee, telling a young Jewish girl, Mary, that she would be the mother of the Son of God. What a way to get the news!

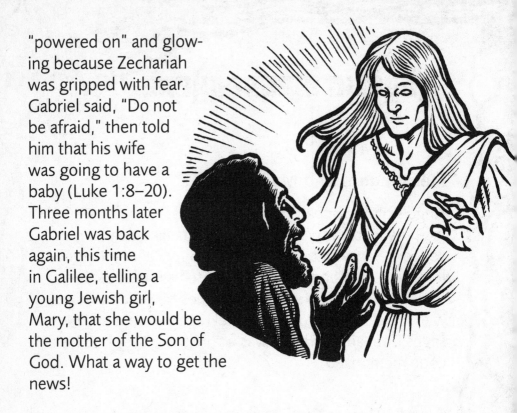

Leave Bethlehem! Tonight!

After the Wise Men had come and gone, Joseph and Mary tucked baby Jesus in his bed and turned in for the night. Nothing unusual so far. But in the middle of the night, an angel appeared to Joseph in a dream and told him to get up—and now. The angel said he had to hightail it to Egypt as quickly as possible. The angel said that King Herod wanted to kill Jesus. Joseph woke Mary; they bundled up the baby, grabbed their donkey, and split. Herod's soldiers came around the next day, but Joseph and his family were gone. They stayed in Egypt till the angel visited again and told them it was okay to go home (Matthew 2:13–21).

Angel Gives Traffic Directions

One day when Philip was minding his own business, an angel of the Lord suddenly said to him, "Go south to the road—the desert road—that goes down from Jerusalem to Gaza." So Philip was out the door, out the city gate, and gone. He had no idea why he was going out to a highway in the desert, but God knew and the angel knew too. Turned out there was an important official from Ethiopia traveling that road. The Ethiopian wanted to know more about God. Philip met him, told him about Jesus, and the man became a Christian (Acts 8:26–38).

"Lost at Sea." Wait, Maybe Not!

Paul and 275 people were on a ship sailing for Rome when a wind of hurricane force hit them. The storm raged for fourteen days and it was so dark they couldn't see the sun. Whoa! Talk about seasick! They were sure they were doomed. Then Paul looked and there was some guy he'd never seen before standing beside him. Now where did he come from? Turns out the guy was an angel come to say that God was going to rescue them, that no one would be hurt, and that the ship would run aground on an island (Acts 27). Paul told everyone about the angel's message, and shortly after, that's exactly what happened.

Explaining Stuff

Sometimes when God sent a vision or a dream, he also
sent an angel to explain what it meant. For example, Daniel
had a really wild vision of bizarre beasts. You can bet he
was happy to wake up and find out it was all a dream. He
was also happy to have someone explain what it all meant
(Daniel 7:16; 10:14). Angels also explained stuff to the
prophet Zechariah (Zechariah 1:9, 19) and the apostle John
(Revelation 17). If you'd had a vision of a four-headed leop-
ard, colored horses, or a seven-headed dragon, you'd probably appreciate an explanation too.

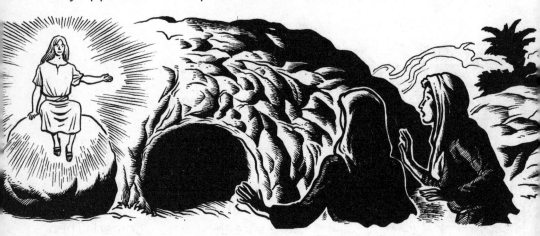

He's Not Here, Ladies

When Jesus was raised from the dead, an angel rolled away
the mammoth stone from his tomb, then sat down on it
(Matthew 28:2). When some women came to the tomb,
the angel explained to them that Jesus was no longer in the
tomb. He had risen from the dead. A little while later some
more women came and this time two angels met them and
gave them the same message (Luke 24:1–7). Hey! Telling

the good news is our job now but the angels got the ball rolling—and the stone too.

He'll Be Back

Just before Jesus rose into heaven, he said we should go and tell everyone about him, but then when Jesus ascended up into heaven, the disciples were still standing there with their heads leaned back, mouths open, looking up, and wondering, "Uh ... now what?" Suddenly two angels appeared and asked why they were still standing there. Kind of like a construction foreman coming around to say, "Hey, stop leaning on the shovels. Get back to work" (Acts 1:10–11).

get deeper

In the Bible, God led and directed his people by talking to them, giving them dreams and visions, sending angels, sending angels in dreams and visions, giving a message through a leader, sending signs, giving people wise counselors, and sometimes by using circumstances. Each time the message and the method seemed unique. When we trust God, he will direct and lead us, but the way he does it is up to him. Thank God each day for his guidance and direction.

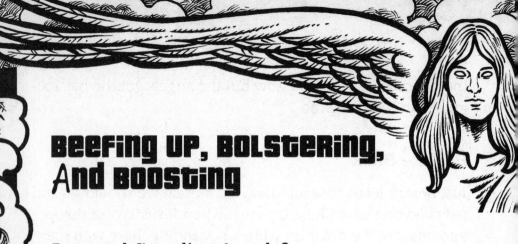

Beefing Up, Bolstering, And Boosting

Personal Guardian Angels?

Many Christians believe that each of us has a guardian angel assigned to us. What does the Bible say? When Jesus was talking about kids once, he said, "I tell you that their angels in heaven always see the face of my Father in heaven" (Matthew 18:10). So kids have angels. And then what happens when they grow up? Do the angels leave them? Not likely. Psalm 91:9–11 says that if you make the Most High your dwelling place (your home) ... he will command his angels to take care of you. We don't know for sure if we have one personal angel who is a bodyguard, or if God sends a different angel each time we need help. All we know is that when we trust in God, he will make sure angels are there to help us.

Angels with Emotions

Sometimes we think angels go around doing their job like robots without any emotions or feelings. But the prophet Zechariah had a vision where an angel got so upset at the terrible condition of the Jews that he asked, "Lord Almighty, how long will you withhold mercy from Jerusalem ... which you have been angry with these seventy years?" In other words, the angel said to God,

"How long are you going to let this go on? I know you were angry, but ..." God cared about the angel's emotions and feelings. He "spoke kind and comforting words to the angel" (Zechariah 1:12–13).

Angels not only get sad when bad stuff happens, but they get very, very happy when good stuff happens—like when people believe in Jesus and are saved. Luke 15:10 says, "There is rejoicing in the presence of the angels of God over one sinner who repents." Yeah! Party time!

Help That Weakling!

Daniel had been fasting for three weeks when he saw an angel. He was so weak from not eating that he collapsed right on his face on the ground. Whump! First the angel pulled him up on his hands and knees. Daniel said, "My strength is gone and I can hardly breathe." Daniel didn't have asthma. He was just beat.

So the angel touched him, gave him strength, and said, "Be strong now!" And he was. Instantly! (Daniel 10) Wow! If getting strong was always this easy you'd never need to exercise. (But don't count on it.)

Angels Looking After Jesus

Jesus fasted for forty days. At the end of the fast he was getting so hungry he was practically looking at rocks as food and licking his lips. That's when Satan attacked Jesus full force—at his very weakest, tempting him to turn those rocks into real bread. But Jesus refused to listen. He refused to turn even one bitsy bit of gravel into a teeny bun. "Then the devil left him, and angels came and attended him" (Matthew 4:1–11). We don't know if the angels cooked Jesus a meal like they had for Elijah, or if they simply gave him enough strength to get to town and order lunch. No matter, they did take care of him.

Another time when Jesus was praying, the Bible says he was in anguish and "his sweat was like drops of blood falling to the ground." At that time an angel from heaven appeared and strengthened him (Luke 22:39–44). Jesus had always known that angels were a part of God's plan for him. He once told Nathanael he would see "the angels of God ascending and descending on the Son of Man" (John 1:51).

get stronger

There were times when angels supernaturally strengthened people who were weak. Other times the angels helped them go without food. There may be times in your life when you're doing God's work and he sends an angel to strengthen you. It's not going to work, however, if you stay up till the wee hours on a school night eating nothing but junk food and watching TV, and then expect God to give you the strength to get to school the next day. God wants you to take care of your body, eat properly, and to get enough sleep and exercise.

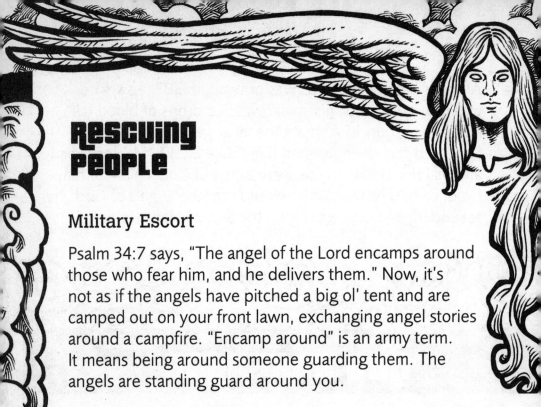

Rescuing People

Military Escort

Psalm 34:7 says, "The angel of the Lord encamps around those who fear him, and he delivers them." Now, it's not as if the angels have pitched a big ol' tent and are camped out on your front lawn, exchanging angel stories around a campfire. "Encamp around" is an army term. It means being around someone guarding them. The angels are standing guard around you.

Escape from Sodom

When a city full of thousands of men crowd the streets surrounding your house, wanting to beat you into the dust, how do you escape? That is the question Lot had on his mind. The entire population of Sodom wanted to attack him and his guests, who happened to be angels. The angels stretched out their hands and ... ZAAAAPP! ... struck all the men blind. After that, since the men couldn't see him, it was pretty easy for Lot to run through the city to warn his sons-in-law. He just had to dodge thousands of blind men who were staggering around bumping into each other. (Kluuuunk! Oh yeah, and into walls too.) The angels slept over at Lot's house that night. The next morning, they led Lot and his family out of the city (Genesis 19:4–16). Piece of cake.

Lion's Den

Daniel faithfully prayed to God even when there was a law against praying. As a result, he was chucked into a den full of starving lions. The reason he didn't get eaten alive was because God sent an angel to shut the lions' mouths (Daniel 6:22). The den was a lion pit where lions lived all the time and chewed people up. It probably wasn't cleaned because no one dared go in to clean it. (Too bad they didn't know Daniel was

going to survive the night or they could've sent him down with a shovel and a broom.) Although Daniel wasn't hurt, he may have come out of there stinking like the bottom of a lion's cage in a zoo. Hey! God did the miracle and kept Daniel safe. Right? But when it came to hygiene, Daniel needed a bath and he had to do the scrubbing.

An Angel Behind a Mass Jailbreak

After Jesus went back to heaven, the high priest Caiaphas had the apostles thrown in jail. The next morning when officers went to get them, they found the jail securely locked (as it should be) with the guards standing at the doors (as they should be). But when they opened the door, there was no one inside! How'd the apostles get out? Easy. During the night an angel opened the doors. Apparently the angel had a sense of humor because after he let them out, he locked the doors again (Acts 5:17–25).

Peter Sprung from Prison

Herod Antipas arrested the apostle Peter, but at night when Peter was locked in chains in an inner prison in total darkness, an angel, shining like a light bulb, woke him. He struck Peter on the side ("Ouch!") and told him, "Quick! Get up!" "Yeah, but these chains ..." Chains nothing. Ka-twannnng! The chains fell off. Peter was so groggy that the angel had to remind him to get dressed. He then led Peter out past all the guards—who didn't even see them! The iron gate swung open and they just walked away into the city (Acts 12:6–11, 18–19).

WARRIOR Angels

Did you know that heaven has an army? Sure, heaven is peaceful and wonderful, but remember, the angels have to battle Satan and his demons. So they're in an army and that army has a commander. When Joshua was about to attack Jericho he saw a man in front of him with a drawn sword. Joshua asked, "Are you for us or for our enemies?" "Neither," he replied, "but as commander of the army of the Lord I have now come" (Joshua 5:13–14).

When the Arameans surrounded the Israelite city of Dothan, Elisha and his servant looked out over the walls and saw that hundreds and hundreds of horses and chariots had surrounded the city. Elisha told his servant not to worry. Then the servant's eyes were opened and he "saw the hills full of horses and chariots of fire all around Elisha" (2 Kings 6:15–17). The Bible doesn't say how many angel chariots were protecting Dothan that day, but Psalm 68:17 says, "The chariots of God are tens of thousands and thousands of thousands." (Thousands of thousands means millions, by the way.) Were the Arameans outgunned? Oh yeaaah.

Does God's army have cavalry units—you know, mounted horsemen? Sure sounds like it. In Revelation 19:11–16,

Jesus is described as riding a great white horse, headed out to battle, and the armies of heaven were following him on white horses. It even looks as if God has angels who ride around on horseback patrols—sort of like angel rangers. The prophet Zechariah had a vision of an angel riding a red horse, and behind him were more angels on horses. God sent these guys riding through all the earth to keep the peace (Zechariah 1:8–11).

What kind of weapons do angels have? Well, Genesis 3:24 says that the cherubim guarding the garden of Eden had a "flaming sword flashing back and forth." Cool! Like a light saber in some sci-fi movie. Balaam once saw the angel of the Lord with his sword drawn (Numbers 22:31). King David also saw the angel of the Lord with a drawn sword in his hand (1 Chronicles 21:16, 27, 30). Now, some people say those swords aren't real swords—they're just symbols of the angel's power.

Who knows? But whatever those weapons were, David, Balaam, Adam, and Eve knew the angel meant business. They weren't about to mess around to find out if the swords were real or not.

Nations have built big impressive armies and navies and air forces, but one thing's for sure, not a single one of them could stand against the armies of heaven.

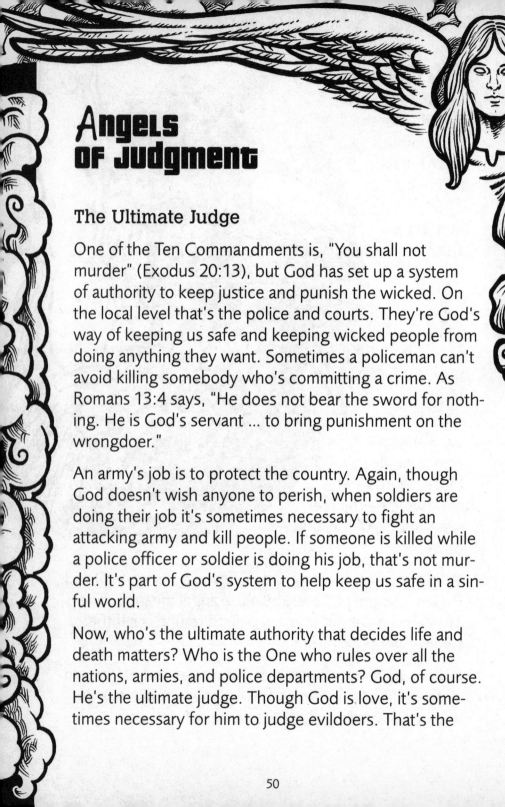

Angels of Judgment

The Ultimate Judge

One of the Ten Commandments is, "You shall not murder" (Exodus 20:13), but God has set up a system of authority to keep justice and punish the wicked. On the local level that's the police and courts. They're God's way of keeping us safe and keeping wicked people from doing anything they want. Sometimes a policeman can't avoid killing somebody who's committing a crime. As Romans 13:4 says, "He does not bear the sword for nothing. He is God's servant ... to bring punishment on the wrongdoer."

An army's job is to protect the country. Again, though God doesn't wish anyone to perish, when soldiers are doing their job it's sometimes necessary to fight an attacking army and kill people. If someone is killed while a police officer or soldier is doing his job, that's not murder. It's part of God's system to help keep us safe in a sinful world.

Now, who's the ultimate authority that decides life and death matters? Who is the One who rules over all the nations, armies, and police departments? God, of course. He's the ultimate judge. Though God is love, it's sometimes necessary for him to judge evildoers. That's the way he holds back evil and rescues good people—and the Bible tells of times when God used his angels to execute that judgment.

A Band of Destroying Angels

The Israelites were slaves in Egypt. Merciless taskmasters worked them and whipped them, driving them until they dropped. God tried everything to convince Pharaoh to let his people go, but Pharaoh refused. So one night God sent a band of destroying angels around to every house in Egypt (Psalm 78:49–51). Only they weren't like security guards checking doors, making sure everyone was safe. They were angels of death, and since the Egyptians were fighting God, the angels went in and killed the firstborn in every house (Exodus 12:29–30). Pharaoh then changed his mind and let the people of Israel go.

Angels with Plague-Swords

Hundreds of years after the destroyer angels passed through Egypt, the angel of the Lord pulled out his plague-sword in Israel. King David became proud and disobeyed God. So the death angel went all over Israel killing people. By the time he stopped at Jerusalem, 70,000 people had died (2 Samuel 24:13–16). A few hundred years later, the angel of the Lord came back to Jerusalem with his death-sword drawn. Only this time the target was the Assyrian army that was camped around the city ready to attack. In one night, this angel killed 185,000 men in the Assyrian camp (2 Kings 19:35). That's like killing everyone in a city the size of Des Moines, Iowa.

Worms for Weapons

It's cool to have a flaming angel-sword like the cherubim, but have you ever heard of the angel who used worms as a weapon? After King Herod Agrippa killed the apostle James, he became super proud. Then, "an angel of the Lord struck him down, and he was eaten by worms and died" (Acts 12:23).

get deeper

When we're God's child, we're forgiven, and God helps us live as Christians. When we're trying our best and growing in our understanding, we'll still make mistakes, but we don't need to worry. God loves us a lot and is patient and never gives up on us. He already knows we're not perfect. But sometimes people think that being forgiven means they can live any way they want. They think it is all right to willfully sin against God. They think God will turn a blind eye and not care that they're purposely breaking his laws. Wow! Are they in for a surprise! Galatians 6:7 warns: "Do not be deceived: God cannot be mocked. A man reaps what he sows." You see, God knows that his way of doing things really works. He also knows that sin destroys and hurts others and us. Yes, God loves us, but to keep everyone safe he judges sin. We should never assume we can get away with doing whatever we want.

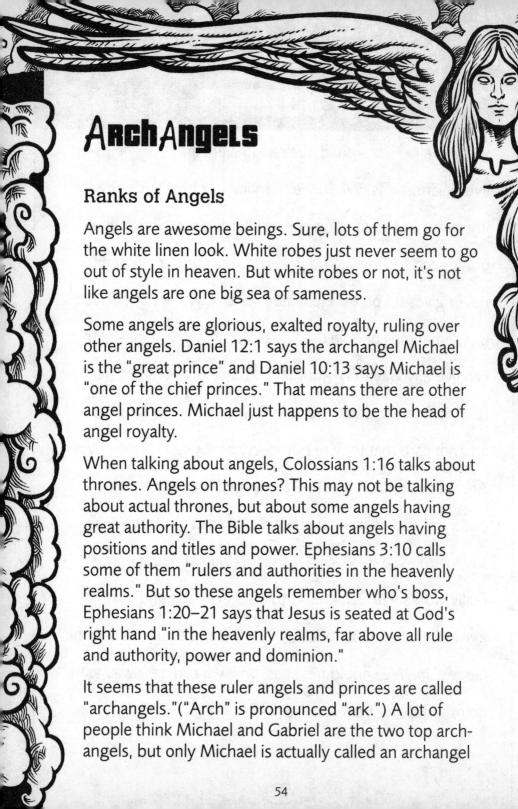

ArchAngels

Ranks of Angels

Angels are awesome beings. Sure, lots of them go for the white linen look. White robes just never seem to go out of style in heaven. But white robes or not, it's not like angels are one big sea of sameness.

Some angels are glorious, exalted royalty, ruling over other angels. Daniel 12:1 says the archangel Michael is the "great prince" and Daniel 10:13 says Michael is "one of the chief princes." That means there are other angel princes. Michael just happens to be the head of angel royalty.

When talking about angels, Colossians 1:16 talks about thrones. Angels on thrones? This may not be talking about actual thrones, but about some angels having great authority. The Bible talks about angels having positions and titles and power. Ephesians 3:10 calls some of them "rulers and authorities in the heavenly realms." But so these angels remember who's boss, Ephesians 1:20–21 says that Jesus is seated at God's right hand "in the heavenly realms, far above all rule and authority, power and dominion."

It seems that these ruler angels and princes are called "archangels."("Arch" is pronounced "ark.") A lot of people think Michael and Gabriel are the two top arch-angels, but only Michael is actually called an archangel

(Jude v. 9). Gabriel is simply called an angel (Luke 1:19, 26). Mind you, "archangel" means "chief messenger" and Gabriel did act as a chief messenger when he brought the good news about Jesus being born.

Name: Michael

Meaning: Who is like God?

Titles: Great Prince, Archangel, the Great Prince Who Protects the People of God

Birth Date: Not born; created before the world began

Address: Heaven

Positions Held: Chief Messenger of heaven to earth; highest-ranking military angel, head of the Army of God—including but not limited to: army, chariot divisions, cavalry units

Major Accomplishments: Defeated the demon Prince of Persia in hand-to-hand combat; provided ongoing protection of God's people till present time

Future Plans: To take a strong stand during the final time of great trouble, to defeat Satan in the final all-out battle

Famous Quotes: "The Lord rebuke you!" (Jude v.9).

Name: Gabriel

Meaning: Man of God

Titles: Angel

Birth Date: Like Michael, created before the dawn of time

Address: Heaven

Positions Held: Messenger, Teacher of Prophets

Major Accomplishments: Explained mysteries to Daniel; supported and protected Darius the Mede; informed Zacharias that his wife would give birth to a boy named John; delivered news of Jesus' birth to Mary

Future Plans: Defeat evil, help people

Famous Quotes: "I am Gabriel. I stand in the presence of God" (Luke 1:19).

the
INCREDIBLE cherubim

Cherubim are a race of incredible spiritual beings, and when you're talking about only one of them, it's a cherub. The problem is, when you say "cherub" people automatically think of pudgy baby angels with stubby white wings—innocent Cupids shooting love arrows into people. They fly around in diapers that look like they're about to fall off. (Ohhhh, cuuuute!) Not. Not. Not. That is a totally wrong picture of a cherub. In mythology, Cupid was no innocent little angel. He was the pagan, cruel Roman 'god' of sex. The Romans used to draw Cupid as a man who mistreated his wife. After a while they switched to images of him as a chubby toddler. So don't think of pictures of little cupids when you think of God's cherubim.

Here's the real scoop. The Bible calls cherubim "beasts" (Revelation 4:6 KJV). In the New International Version (NIV), they're called "creatures." Why such bizarre names? What are they? They're beings with huge monster bodies, wings all over the place—six per creature—and eyeballs covering their bodies. (Which means they don't roll around in the mud.) And that's just their bodies. Their faces are another matter. They have four faces—one face like a man, another like an ox, another like a lion, and the last like an eagle.

Actually cherubim show up two different ways. When Ezekiel was down by the Kebar River in Babylon in 592 BC, in a vision, he saw cherubim around God's throne. Each cherub had four faces (man, ox, lion, and eagle), and each had four wings. They had hands like a man's hands, but calf's feet that gleamed like polished bronze (Ezekiel 1:5–11). You gotta admit, that is bizarre.

Then, 680 years later, the apostle John also saw the cherubim. They still had eyeballs all over—which is quite cool—only this time they had six wings instead of four. And instead of each beast having four faces, each beast had one face. Now one beast was like a lion, one was like an ox, the third had a face like a man, and the fourth was like an eagle (Revelation 4:6–8). Weird, huh? Do they morph right in front of you? Or are there different kinds of cherubim and they take turns guarding the throne? It's one of those things we won't know till we get to heaven.

The cherubim sit around God's throne praising him non-stop, day and night like his personal praise and worship team (Revelation 4:8). But they also seem to be like some kind of honor guards. Powerful? You bet. You definitely wanna take them seriously. Ezekiel 1:13–14 says, "The appearance of the living creatures was like burning coals of fire or like torches ... The creatures sped back and forth like flashes of lightning." That's probably when they're powered up.

Psalm 18:10 says even God rides these flying monsters: "He mounted the cherubim and flew; he soared on the wings of the wind." Wow! Can you imagine going for a ride on one of those flying monsters? Whooo-eeeee! Cherubim are also armed and dangerous. Cherubim with a flaming sword guarded the garden of Eden so Adam and Eve couldn't sneak back in (Genesis 3:24).

God told the Israelites to carve golden cherubim on top of the ark of the covenant. Just like the kings of old used to carve golden lions around their thrones, God wanted to show that some pretty awesome beasts surrounded his throne as well.

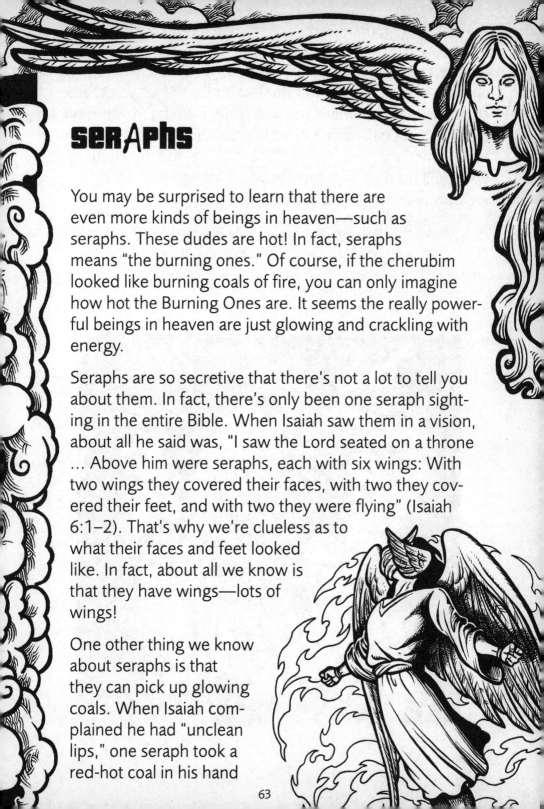

SERAPHS

You may be surprised to learn that there are even more kinds of beings in heaven—such as seraphs. These dudes are hot! In fact, seraphs means "the burning ones." Of course, if the cherubim looked like burning coals of fire, you can only imagine how hot the Burning Ones are. It seems the really powerful beings in heaven are just glowing and crackling with energy.

Seraphs are so secretive that there's not a lot to tell you about them. In fact, there's only been one seraph sighting in the entire Bible. When Isaiah saw them in a vision, about all he said was, "I saw the Lord seated on a throne … Above him were seraphs, each with six wings: With two wings they covered their faces, with two they covered their feet, and with two they were flying" (Isaiah 6:1–2). That's why we're clueless as to what their faces and feet looked like. In fact, about all we know is that they have wings—lots of wings!

One other thing we know about seraphs is that they can pick up glowing coals. When Isaiah complained he had "unclean lips," one seraph took a red-hot coal in his hand

and put it up to Isaiah's mouth! (Isaiah 6:5–7) Maybe that's standard practice where seraphs come from but it was new to Isaiah! Since he didn't howl in pain, this had to be spiritual. In fact, the seraph said, "See, this has touched your lips; your guilt is taken away and your sin atoned for." Seraphs are holy and very powerful beings.

And that's it. That's all we know about seraphs. You thought cherubim were mysterious? Ha! Seraphs are even more secretive!

get stronger

In science fiction, imaginary aliens usually look very weird, but the funny thing is, they think they're normal and that we look very weird. When we read the descriptions of fantastic creatures God created like cherubim, seraphs, and archangels, we might think, "Wow! They're really cool!" or "Whew! They're kind of weird." But all those amazing creatures may be looking at us and thinking, "Wow! They're God's children, made in his image!" Even though we may look in the mirror and not think much of what we see, it's still true that the bodies God gave us are truly extraordinary and work in an almost miraculous way. We need not only to be thankful for them, just the way they are, but to honor God by taking care of them. We need to keep ourselves healthy and fit, and be the best that we can be.

the Angel of the Lord

Give Me Some Skin!

God does not have a physical body like we do. He is a spirit. But since he is God, he can appear in a physical form if he chooses to. And he did appear several times! Often the Bible talks about an incredible being, "the Angel of the Lord," appearing to someone. The next thing you know he's saying, "I am God." Like when the Angel of the Lord appeared to Moses in the burning bush and then "God called to him from within the bush" (Exodus 3:2–4).

Angel (malak) in Hebrew means "messenger," and sometimes the Bible uses that word when talking about an ordinary human messenger, not necessarily an angel. So the "Angel of the Lord" is a messenger of God. And since this Angel talks like he's God, most people believe that he is God himself. In fact, since Jesus has always lived with God as the second person of the Trinity, many Christians think that this was Jesus coming to earth before he was born in a physical body.

If the Bible talks about "an" angel, chances are good it's just a regular angel. But whenever it speaks of "the" Angel of the Lord, sit up straight and pay extra special attention. Let's read about some times when the Angel of the Lord came to earth.

God Drops by Abraham's Tent

One hot, sunshiny day, three "men" come strolling along and show up at Abraham's tent. Abraham offered them lunch, so the men sat down, chowed down, and talked with him. Then one of them—whom the Bible calls "the Lord"—said ninety-year-old Sarah would have a son. As they leave, this guy told Abraham that he's about to destroy the entire city of Sodom. In fact, he's gonna wipe all four cities of the plain off the map. Abraham's eyebrows go up. He clues in that he's talking with God himself. The other two men? Seems they were just ordinary angels (Genesis 18:1–19:1).

Wrestling with God

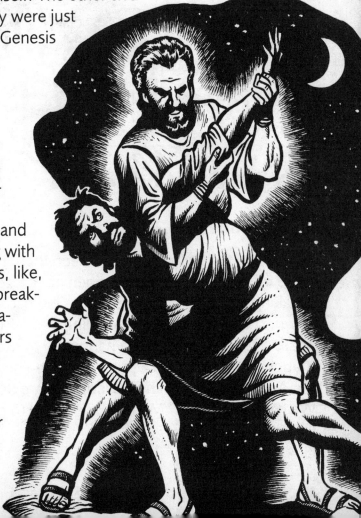

One night Jacob was praying desperately when a man showed up and started wrestling with him. ("Hey! I was, like, praying. You're breaking my concentration.") After hours of using his best wrestling holds, Jacob clued in that this stranger was God. At sunrise both Jacob and the stranger were all sweaty and the stranger said, "You have struggled with God ... and have overcome." Jacob called that spot Peniel ("Face of God"), saying, "I saw God face to face, and yet my life was spared" (Genesis 32:22–32). Talk about escaping death, buddy; you not only saw God, you tried to trip him and throw him to the ground.

It's a Prophet! No, It's God!

When God talked to Gideon, Gideon thought he was just some other man. He freaked when he realized he was speaking to the Angel of the Lord. God had to calm him down: "Peace! ... You are not going to die." ("Oh, whew! That's a relief!") Same thing happened to Manoah. At first he thought the "man" was a prophet. When he realized it was the Angel of the Lord, he wailed, "We are doomed to die! ... We have seen God!" Manoah's wife had to calm him down (Judges 6:11–23; 13:1–23).

get COOLeR

The Angel of the Lord paid a visit to men like Abraham, Jacob, Moses, and Gideon. We think, "Wow! They must have been pretty incredible and holy guys to get a personal visit." But those visits didn't have as much to do with them, as they had to do with how God wanted to work through them to accomplish his plans and bless others. As a boy growing into a man of God, live your life caring about how to help others. God's kingdom needs your help in making this world a better place in which to live. Yes, God cares for us, but he also wants to use our lives to help care for others.

SATAN FALLS BIG TIME

Satan (a.k.a. Diablos, the Devil, Lucifer)

When you're talking villains, there are some guys so utterly wicked that they make the worst bad guy you've seen in a movie seem like nothing more than a schoolyard bully.

In the New Testament, diamonion means devils—the regular run-of-the-mill demons—but Diabolos means Satan, the Devil, the head honcho of all the devils. The Devil has lots of names and none of them are good. Satan means "the hater, accuser," and he's called "the accuser of our brothers" (Revelation 12:10). He's also called "the great dragon ... that ancient serpent called the devil, or Satan, who leads the whole world astray" (Revelation 12:9). He's also called "Beelzebub, the prince of demons" (Matthew 12:24). "Beelzebub" means "lord of flies." Some name, huh? You know what kind of stuff flies are usually attracted to.

Some Bible scholars think that Ezekiel 28:2, 12–17 (which talks about the king of Tyre), and Isaiah 14:12–15 (which talks about the king of Babylon) are also talking about Satan and his fall from heaven. If that's the case, then here's the startling picture we see.

In the beginning Satan was not the deformed, dragon-like monstrosity that he is pictured as being today. In fact, next to God, he was the coolest dude in heaven. Not only cool, but "the model of perfection, full of wisdom and perfect in beauty" (Ezekiel 28:12). He was a guardian cherub—remember one of those awesome winged creatures surrounding God's throne?

His clothes were something else! Not only gold, but also every kind of precious stone adorned him: ruby, topaz, emerald, chrysolite, onyx, jasper, sapphire, turquoise, and beryl. If you've ever seen a picture of Elvis Presley in his rhinestone suit, that's barely a shadow of Satan all decked out.

Picture this perfect, wise, beautiful cherub in Eden decked out with glittering gems. Perfect? Oh yeah. Satan was blameless in his ways, but then he became proud of his beauty. His problem? He looked in too many mirrors and saw what a good-looking guy he was—and in his pride he said, "I will make myself like the Most High" (Isaiah 14:14).

What happened? Did he get a shot at the throne? Nope. God had Michael dump him into the elevator and press the "H" button for the bottom floor. Jesus saw it happen. He later said, "I saw Satan fall like lightning from heaven" (Luke 10:18). Like lightning? Whew! Sounds like they wanted the Devil outta there fast!

next stop, Hades

Going Down!

When he got the boot and fell like lightning, where did the Devil land? On earth. That's why he's called "the prince of this world" (John 14:30). And he had quite a crowd with him. About a third of the angels did the demon dive with him (Revelation 12:7-9). It's hard to imagine why millions of angels would have believed Satan instead of God when they had it so good in heaven. But they did. Jude verse 6 says they had positions of authority in heaven, yet they threw them away. They had a fabulous place to live but they abandoned their own home.

The Devil's Dumb Dream

When his rebellion in heaven failed, Satan tried to be a "god" here on earth. That's why 2 Corinthians 4:4 calls him "the god of this age." Demons just love to deceive people into worshiping them as gods. Satan tried to get Jesus to fall down and worship him and Paul said plainly that the "gods" of the pagans were really—you guessed it—demons! (Matthew 4:8–10; 1 Corinthians 10:20). They just never got over wanting to be worshiped as gods.

The Abyss/Tartarus/ The Pit

When Satan's angels rebelled, God bound the worst of them with everlasting chains, chucking them into gloomy, dark dungeons in an extremely deep place in hades called Tartarus or the Pit. Now, Tartarus is not a place where you sit and eat tarts. It's like Alcatraz for evil spirits, the maximum-security prison for demons—and none of them ever break out. It's also called the Abyss (Luke 8:31) and old Bible translations call it the "bottomless pit" (Revelation 9:1 KJV). Scary place to get dropped. Yaaaaagh!

The Devil's Current Address

A few devils were locked up, but millions of them were allowed to stay free and serve Satan. They live behind the scenes in dark spiritual realms, in the world of the dead called "hades." (That's hay-deez.) Different than the Abyss—the prison for evil spirits. When Jesus died for our sins he defeated Satan and he now holds the keys of death and hades (Revelation 1:18).

According to Jesus' story about Lazarus and the rich man, when the unsaved die, they go first into hades. (The word used for "hell" in Luke 16:19–31 is hades, not the lake of fire.) At the final judgment, just before God makes the heaven and the earth new again, hades will be emptied out and everyone judged. Then Satan, his demons, and anyone whose name is not found in the book of life will be thrown into the lake of fire (Revelation 20:13–15).

What Do Demons Look Like?

Satan went from a beautiful cherub to a snaky dragon called the Devil. What about the angels that fell with him? What did they look like after they became demons? The Bible doesn't say much about this, but it's a sure bet they weren't entering any beauty contests. John once saw demons that looked like frogs (Revelation 16:13–14). Lots of cartoons show demons with red skin, a pointy tail, and horns, but the Bible doesn't say that.

One Lake of Fire Comin' Up!

Some time after the demons rebelled, God created a very nasty place in the spiritual dimension for their final punishment. It's called the lake of fire, a.k.a. the lake of burning sulfur. This place is worse than hades and the Abyss. It was originally designed with the Devil and his demons in mind. In Matthew 25:41 Jesus called it "eternal fire prepared for the Devil and his angels." At the end of the world, Satan and his demons will definitely go off the deep end into the lake

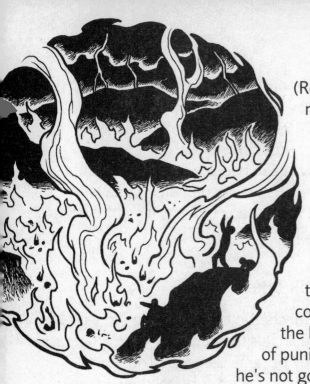

(Revelation 20:10, 15). But not only demons will go there, so will wicked people.

You've probably seen cartoons of the Devil with a red cape and a pitchfork, cracking a whip over people while they shovel burning coals in hell. Not! When the Devil goes to his place of punishment, the lake of fire, he's not going to be ruling over anyone. He's going to be one of the inmates and he'll be squealing like a lobster in a burning sulfur cooker.

Shuddering with Fear

Do the demons know about this final place of torment? You bet they do! Jesus said, "Be afraid of the One who can destroy both soul and body in hell." And the demons are scared! They're scared absolutely silly. They're literally shuddering (Matthew 10:28; James 2:19). If they were wearing armor you could hear it rattling.

Don't Send Us to the Abyss!

One day Jesus met two demon-possessed men and the demons living in them shouted, "Have you come here to torture us before the appointed time? Swear to God that you won't torture me!" (Matthew 8:29; Mark 5:7). In about, oh, one minute they stopped trying to tell Jesus what to do and began whimpering. "And they begged him repeatedly not to order them to go into the Abyss" (Luke 8:31). Remember, the Abyss is the Pit, the prison where some evil spirits are locked up. Bad as it is, it's not even the final punishment. The lake of fire is the end of the line. So the demons have lots to be scared about—the Slammer and the Cooker.

get cooler

How did the demons fall? When they were created, all angels were created holy. They were innocent. Even Satan was perfect in all his ways until he became proud. But after they sinned and a third of the angels rebelled with Satan (Revelation 12:4), God kicked them out. That would be millions of angels. To convince all those angels, the Devil must really have believed in his cause. Which goes to show, even if millions of others are doing something wrong, that still doesn't make it okay for you to do it. Just because there are those who are convincing and very persuasive, doesn't mean you should follow them. Be like the noble Bereans (Acts 17:11). Read, learn, and follow what God has shown us in his Word, the Bible.

SAtAn's EViL GAme PLAn

Misery Loves Company

What's Satan's ultimate goal? Well, he'd still like to be like God, but he knows that ain't gonna happen. Next on his wish list, he'd really, really like to avoid getting heaved into the lake of burning sulfur, but he's going whether he likes it or not. So he figures if he has to go to hell, he'll take as many people with him as possible. He tries to get people to disbelieve God and live wicked lives so that they end up there too. God loves people and doesn't want to see anyone perish (2 Peter 3:9).

Satan's Game Plan

"The devil prowls around like a roaring lion looking for someone to devour" (1 Peter 5:8). He wants humans to be miserable, so he lies to them and tries to keep them from God's truth. He tries to stop them from living God's way. Result? They're miserable. But Satan's ultimate goal is to prevent them from accepting Jesus Christ, because he doesn't want people to live with God in heaven. He wants them to end up in the lake of burning sulfur with him.

The Father of Lies

Jesus said about the Devil: "There is no truth in him. When he lies, he speaks his native language, for he is a liar and the father of lies" (John 8:44). He told his first lie to Eve. He first made her question the truth by saying, "Did God really say ...?" Then once he had her questioning God's truth, he out-and-out lied to her (Genesis 3:1–5). Satan is the father of lies. He's the best liar there is. He invented lying. He even lied to Jesus trying to deceive him. Jesus didn't fall for it (Matthew 4:5–7), but the Devil is still using lies as his main weapon today. The Bible also says he has "blinded the minds of unbelievers" (2 Corinthians 4:4). He does that by causing them to question the truth and believe his lies.

Demonic Teachers

Since Christians believe the Bible, the Devil quotes it to them trying to influence them—except that he twists verses, turning true doctrine into false doctrine. This is called distorting the scriptures (2 Peter 3:16). As 1 Timothy 4:1 says, he tries to get people to "follow deceiving spirits and things taught by demons." Wow! You sure don't want a demon to teach you. Right? And Galatians 1:9 says, "If anybody is preaching to you a gospel other than what you accepted, let him be eternally condemned!" One of he surest signs of a cult (those teaching another gospel) is that they deny or rewrite basic Christian doctrine. For example, they'll say that Jesus is not part of the Trinity. Look out when people start saying, "All the other Christians have it wrong. The truth has only been revealed to us." When the Devil tried to deceive

Jesus he used Bible verses. He's still trying to do that today, and some people deceive other people too.

What Can the Devil Do?

The Devil's biggest power and influence is deception. If he can deceive people he can cause them to do all kinds of wicked things that will hurt themselves and others. He wants to keep people out of heaven. If you're a Christian, living God's way and trusting God, you have no reason to fear the Devil. The Devil is not like God. God can be everywhere. The Devil can only be in one place at one time. God knows everything. Satan does not. God can do anything, but the Devil is very limited in what he can or can't do.

Remember the angel who brought a plague as punishment on Israel? Evil angels sometimes use germs and sickness as weapons too (Luke 13:11, 16). "Satan ... afflicted Job with painful sores from the soles of his feet to the top of his head" (Job 2:7). Of course, germs are capable of being nasty all on their own. It's not like they need supernatural help to make you sick. Most of the time you get sick because the kid in the desk next to you spins around and sneezes in your face. Or you just might get sick if you want to show how "tough" you are, so you walk to school in winter with only a T-shirt on. We need to take care of ourselves (a doctor can help with that) and we also need to pray that God will help us be healthy.

The Devil does not have unlimited power over the weather. When tornados rip through Kansas and hurricanes batter Florida, it's not Satan's doing. They're caused by warm air mixing with cold air and … and … well, read about it in your encyclopedia. The Bible only mentions one time when God gave the Devil permission to get his hands on a tornado and steer it in Job's direction (Job 1:12, 18–19).

When the apostle Paul was caught in a shrieking storm for fourteen days, he didn't say, "Oh dear! It's the Devil huffing and puffing!" Acts 27:14 says it was "a wind of hurricane force, called the 'northeaster.'" Bad wind, yeah. Scary, yeah. But nothing supernatural. The wind usually blew that time of year.

Sometimes Satan inspires evil men to cast Christians into prison (Revelation 2:10). But remember, God's angels have sprung people out of prison! Remember, God stands for the truth and Satan stands for lies, so of course the Devil's going to fight the truth. Just know that God is greater than the Devil (1 John 4:4).

get smarter

Demons love to tempt people to sin. They play on things that appeal to people's greed or pride or lust, and they use lies to try to make it seem okay to sin. "Just this one time." "God wouldn't mind that much." "It won't hurt anyone." "It's not really wrong." James 1:14–15 says, "Each one is tempted when, by his own evil desire, he is dragged away and enticed ... and sin, when it is full-grown, gives birth to death." In other words, the Devil can't make you sin. All he can do is lie to you and try to make you believe his lies to the point where you're finally drawn into sin. Paul said we shouldn't be unaware of the Devil's schemes and adds, "Do not give the devil a foothold" (2 Corinthians 2:11; Ephesians 4:27). So when you hear lies in your head or from others about how it would be okay to do what you know is wrong, recognize the Devil's tricks and make a decision right away: "No way! I'm doing things God's way!"

BATTLE in the SPIRITUAL WORLD

WARRiOR
Angels vs. Demons

The Bible talks about Michael and his warrior angels fighting against Satan and his demonic hordes. Imagine Hollywood making a movie about that with out-of-this-world special effects. But it's not just the angels fighting evil. We help in the battle too.

Ephesians 6:12 says, "Our struggle is not against flesh and blood, but against the rulers, against the authorities, against the powers of this dark world and against the spiritual forces of evil in the heavenly realms." In other words, the Devil deceives and blinds people, tempts them with sin, and tries to stop the gospel. So even though we see the evil that people do in the world around us, Paul reminds us about what's really happening. Deceived people don't need to be defeated; they need to be freed. The Devil is the enemy. He's the one who needs to be defeated. Evil people need to be reached, helped, and saved. That's how we fight the Devil and his hordes—by resisting him in our own lives and by praying for and sharing the Good News with lost people.

The angels help while they struggle against these demons too. Are angels scared? Not! Some cartoons show ugly demons with glowing eyeballs and lots of power. You may think that demons are the scary ones.

But remember, it's the good angels with eyes burning with God's power. The Devil and his minions have no real power.

When the evil angels were cast out of heaven, millions of them were not wrapped in chains and locked in the Abyss. They got to move around freely. Satan looked over the available demons and organized them into an army—with a chain of command. Ephesians 6:12 talks about "authorities ... powers of this dark world ... spiritual forces of evil." Colossians 2:15 talks about evil powers and authorities. That may not sound like generals, captains, and sergeants, but that's what it adds up to.

Good angels are not the only ones who have angel princes. Apparently demon princes rule over other demons and over whole nations. When a powerful angel tried to get a message through to Daniel in Persia, the prince of Persia (a demon prince) resisted and battled him for twenty-one days. The angel only broke through enemy lines when Michael showed up to help. After delivering his message, the angel explained that he would have to "return to fight against the prince of Persia" (Daniel 10:12–14; 20). Yeah, that's right. Again.

Revelation 12:7–9 says, "And there was war in heaven. Michael and his angels fought against the dragon (Satan), and the dragon and his angels fought back. But he was not strong enough, and ... he was hurled to the earth, and his angels with him." Ha! And you thought that the Devil was the one always ambushing the angels, while they desperately tried to defend themselves. No way! Here are the angels attacking Satan and his hordes and he is on the defensive—and losing.

You'd be surprised at the things that angels and demons fight over. Deuteronomy 34:5–6 says that when Moses died he was buried somewhere in Moab and "no one knows where his grave is." Well, no person knew, but angels knew, and one day Michael and the Devil were disputing about the body of Moses. (Yes, you read that right. They were arguing over Moses' corpse.) Suddenly Michael pulled out the ultimate weapon. He said, "The Lord rebuke you!" (Jude v. 9). End of argument.

When God's heavenly army goes up against Satan's army, the Devil's troops are no match. First of all, the Devil is only another created being. He can only be in one place at one time. Second, he and all his demons no longer have God's power or a connection to God as God's angels do. Third, if God gets directly involved (God, who has all the power, is everywhere, knows everything and can do anything) the battle is finished right there. And fourth, even if demons were a match for angels, they're outnumbered! Only one-third of the angels went with Satan. Michael still has two-thirds of them—not to mention the seraphs and cherubim and all the Christians here on earth that pray and obey God.

Besides, if you take a peek at the last couple pages of the Bible, you'll see that God has already prophesied a hands-down win for the good guys.

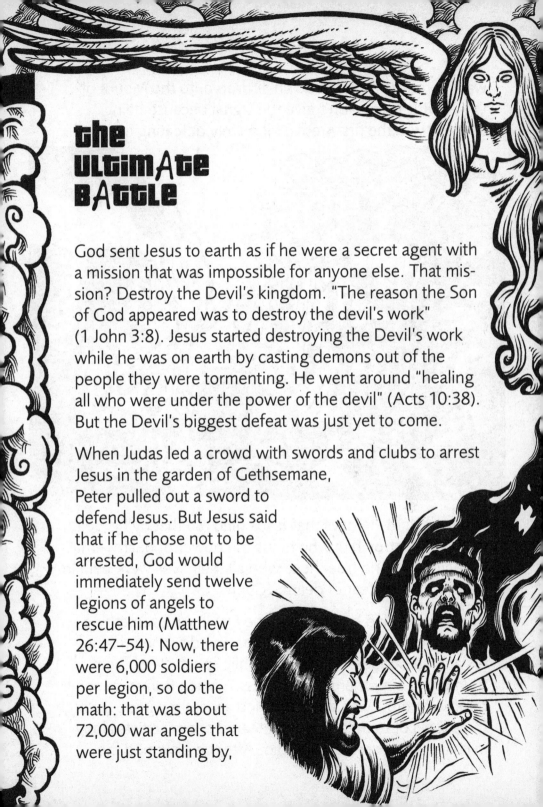

the ULTIMATE BATTLE

God sent Jesus to earth as if he were a secret agent with a mission that was impossible for anyone else. That mission? Destroy the Devil's kingdom. "The reason the Son of God appeared was to destroy the devil's work" (1 John 3:8). Jesus started destroying the Devil's work while he was on earth by casting demons out of the people they were tormenting. He went around "healing all who were under the power of the devil" (Acts 10:38). But the Devil's biggest defeat was just yet to come.

When Judas led a crowd with swords and clubs to arrest Jesus in the garden of Gethsemane, Peter pulled out a sword to defend Jesus. But Jesus said that if he chose not to be arrested, God would immediately send twelve legions of angels to rescue him (Matthew 26:47–54). Now, there were 6,000 soldiers per legion, so do the math: that was about 72,000 war angels that were just standing by, waiting for the signal to do an airdrop onto the Mount of Olives. But Jesus didn't give the signal because being arrested was the first step in ultimately defeating the Devil.

Hebrews 2:14–15 says that Jesus died "so that by his death he might destroy him who holds the power of death—that is, the devil—and free those who all their lives were held in slavery by their fear of death." Cool!

When Jesus died he disarmed the Devil. And something else: Colossians 2:15 says, "And having disarmed the powers and authorities, he made a public spectacle of them, triumphing over them by the cross." When Roman generals returned from a war, they often led a victory parade through the streets of Rome; leading defeated enemy chiefs along in chains. That's what Jesus did. After he disarmed the demons, he made a public spectacle of them. He showed everyone they are powerless and defeated.

Adam and Eve sinned and so did everyone after them. Sin separated all human beings from God. Then the Devil tried to become the god of this world. He tried to control people through sin and deception. When Jesus died for our sins, he defeated the Devil. Now everyone had the opportunity to have sins forgiven, know the truth, and have the one true God as their Father. The only reason why it still looks like the Devil has power, is that although Jesus won the war, each of us still has to choose if we want to serve God or the Devil.

get deeper

Are you glad Jesus died to save you and to defeat the Devil's power in your life? If you believe that Jesus died for your sins, you can pray this prayer: "Dear God, I know I've done bad and selfish things. I'm sorry. Please forgive me. I know your Son Jesus died and was raised from the dead for me. I believe in him. Please make me your child. Please help me love and obey you and learn more about you. In Jesus' name, amen."

If you prayed this prayer sincerely, that is so, so cool! The Devil's kingdom just got smaller, and God's kingdom just got bigger because you moved from the Devil's side to God's side. Now God is your Father, he loves you, and now you're on the winning side!

the BAttLe todAy

The Battle Still Rages

Jesus disarmed Satan's foul, fiendish forces of fear. They can't hurt you. If you're a Christian, no demon can ever come between you and God's love. Paul said, "For I am convinced that neither death nor life, neither angels nor demons ... nor anything else in all creation, will be able to separate us from the love of God that is in Christ Jesus our Lord" (Romans 8:38–39). Until you get to heaven though, you'll still have to defend yourself from the Devil's temptations to sin.

You also need to go on the attack. In the Old Testament, God used the Israelites as his army on earth to bring judgment to sinful nations and to protect God's people in their land. Now we make up God's army. Our weapons are not swords and shields, but the good news about Jesus Christ. The enemy is no longer Canaanites or Assyrians, but sin, the Devil, and his lies. This is the new battleground. We "fight the good fight of the faith" (1 Timothy 6:12).

ARMED FOR bAttle

Even though Jesus broke Satan's power, the Devil still has his army of demons and he's still trying to cause problems. In Ephesians 6:10–17 Paul helped us understand how to fight the good fight of faith. He compared it to a soldier's armor and weapons.

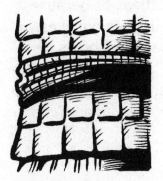

THE BELT OF TRUTH: When we really know God's truth, the Bible, we won't get confused about what is truth and what is lies.

BREASTPLATE OF RIGHTEOUSNESS: Righteousness means having a godly character and living according to God's laws. Jesus forgave our sins. Now we are righteous because of what he did, not because of anything we have done. We keep our breastplate of righteousness in place by doing things God's way. Paul warned us, "Do not give the devil a foothold" (Ephesians 4:27). God doesn't expect us to be perfect, but if we want to keep the Devil from having power in our lives, then we need to stay off his turf. If we blow it and sin, we need to ask God to forgive us. He always will.

SHOES OF READINESS: God wants us to be ready to walk the walk. When we are a Christian example in our communities, we show the world that we believe in Jesus. When people ask why we're different, we can tell them it's because of what Jesus has done in our lives. Soldiers put on their army boots to march into battle. We march into battle every time we share our faith and bring people from the Devil's kingdom into God's kingdom.

SHIELD OF FAITH: Faith means believing in God and always trusting his love. That's important because Satan loves to whisper lies in our ear. When we choose to believe God and not Satan's lies, our shield of faith blocks the flaming arrows of doubts and lies that the Devil shoots at us.

HELMET OF SALVATION: Salvation happens when Jesus delivers us from Satan's power. He gives us salvation when we ask him to forgive our sins and give us eternal life. A helmet protects people's heads; a spiritual helmet protects our souls.

SWORD OF THE SPIRIT: God's Word is our sword. A sword is both an offensive and a defensive weapon, meaning we can use our sword both to defend ourselves against Satan and offensively to attack his lies by speaking truth (Hebrews 4:12). When the Devil tempted Jesus, Jesus responded, "It is written" and quoted God's Word. Truth is the best weapon we have against the Devil's lies. To know the truth we need to know the Bible.

PRAYER: Paul said that we not only need to pray for ourselves and our loved ones closest to us, but also to pray for people like missionaries and ministers who are taking God's Word to the world.

STAND FIRM: First Peter 5:8 says to be alert because "your enemy the devil prowls around like a roaring lion looking for someone to devour. Resist him, standing firm in the faith."

eternity

You want to talk about the ultimate prison? God created the prison of all prisons to hold Satan and his wicked hordes for all eternity. Forget cells and bars! This is like a blazing sea of stinking sulfur.

HeLL:
the Lake OF FiRe

The real name for the lake of fire is Gehenna. This is not hades, but a place of final judgment created for the Devil and his demons. The word Gehenna has quite a history. Just outside the walls of Jerusalem is the Valley of Hinnom (gê-hinnôm in Hebrew). In ancient days, evil kings sacrificed their children to idols there, so the Jews called this valley "the entrance to hell."

Later the Valley of Hinnom was turned into the city's garbage dump. Fires burned garbage all day and all night, and flies crawled on rotten food and meat, laying eggs. The garbage never stopped swarming with millions of maggots. That's why Jesus described hell as a place where "their worm (maggot) does not die, and the fire is not quenched" (Mark 9:48).

The lake of fire is also described as the lake of burning sulfur. Now, sulfur is a foul-smelling yellow powder (like the stink bombs you smell at Fourth of July fireworks) and as the lake burns, a horrible, choking, make-you-gag smoke rises from it. Whoever ends up in the lake is in torment forever and ever. It's so bad that it's called "the second death" (Revelation 14:10–11; 19:20; 20:14). That is where the Devil will be sent.

Is the final judgment actually a lake full of burning sulfur filled with eternal maggots crawling over screaming people—or is this just symbolic? We don't know. But even if it's symbolic, you know it's not symbolizing some nice place. The lake is not like some low-rent suburb of heaven. It is a horrible place to go.

This burning lake (hell) has been designed as the eternal prison for the Devil and his angels (Matthew 25:41).

He'll never be allowed out and will never again have power over anybody. Evil people will be imprisoned in this burning lake with Satan.

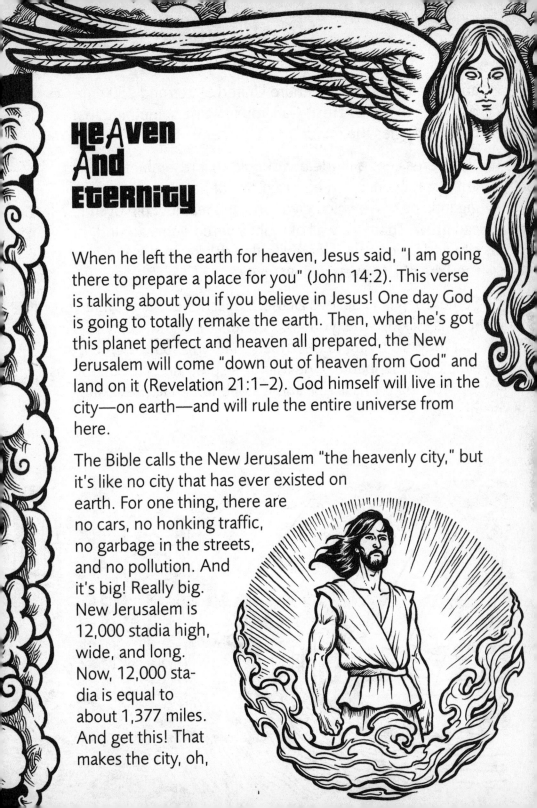

Heaven And Eternity

When he left the earth for heaven, Jesus said, "I am going there to prepare a place for you" (John 14:2). This verse is talking about you if you believe in Jesus! One day God is going to totally remake the earth. Then, when he's got this planet perfect and heaven all prepared, the New Jerusalem will come "down out of heaven from God" and land on it (Revelation 21:1–2). God himself will live in the city—on earth—and will rule the entire universe from here.

The Bible calls the New Jerusalem "the heavenly city," but it's like no city that has ever existed on earth. For one thing, there are no cars, no honking traffic, no garbage in the streets, and no pollution. And it's big! Really big. New Jerusalem is 12,000 stadia high, wide, and long. Now, 12,000 stadia is equal to about 1,377 miles. And get this! That makes the city, oh, about half as big as the entire United States and 250 times higher than Mt. Everest. Can you imagine something that big? It boggles the mind!

New Jerusalem is made out of gold that resembles transparent glass. Even its streets are made of gold. It has gates of gigantic pearls—which gives you an idea how big oysters can grow. There's a wall of multi-layered gems around the city and inside, the river of life flows through this place, with the Tree of Life overshadowing it.

Some Christians believe all these descriptions are "what you read is exactly what you get." Others think they're symbolic; that they are trying to describe something so awesome it's almost indescribable. One thing for sure, the place that Jesus is preparing for us is real and it's phenomenal. (Revelation 21–22.)

Some people think that when we get to heaven we'll just be wispy, misty spiritual thingies floating among the clouds—sort of like floating silk hankies that have brains. Or they fear they'll float around forever on clouds playing harps. (Boooorrrrrring. Maybe that's why they're not too excited about going to heaven. Like, who would want to spend eternity that way?)

The truth is much better! When Jesus returns, we'll be given resurrected, transformed eternal bodies. Will these new bodies be physical or spiritual? They will be both! Our physical bodies will still be physical bodies, only powerful, glorious, imperishable, and immortal (1 Corinthians 15:42–44, 50–54)—like Jesus' body after he rose from the dead.

If you really want to believe heaven is a cloud full of thinking hankies, you can—but like, why would you want to? The truth is so much more exciting!

SMARTER, STRONGER, COOLER, DEEPER—FOREVER!

You've probably heard about "rewards in heaven," but what are these rewards? A lot of people think they're going to get their own palace or mansion. In the King James Version of the Bible, John 14:2 says, "In my Father's house are many mansions." Hmmmm. How can you have mansions inside a house? The New International Version says, "In my Father's house are many rooms." Okay! That makes sense! Of course, God's "house" is a city 1,377 miles high, wide, and long, so the rooms in it could be giganto-normous! Bigger than mansions!

You will be rewarded for the good that you have done on earth. First Corinthians 3:10–14 says that God lays the foundation of salvation, but then, by the way you live your life, you build on that foundation. You either build with gold, silver, costly stones, or with wood, hay, or straw. Sounds like the story of the three little pigs, huh? But this story is for real! If you live your life selfishly, when you arrive in heaven all your wood, hay, and straw deeds will go poof! You'll still be in heaven and mighty glad to be there, but you'll have ashes instead of treasure.

But if you live unselfishly and obey God, your reward will be great. Daniel 12:3 says that obedient believers "will shine ... like the stars for ever and ever" and 1 Corinthians 15:41 says that "star differs from star in splendor." It's your choice: Do you want to live selfishly and end up like a little flickering lightbulb of a star, or live for God and end up with the brightness of a supernova?

Perfect for boys ages 8 to 12, the 2:52 series is based on Luke 2:52: "And Jesus grew in wisdom and stature, and in favor with God and men." Focusing on four primary areas of growth, this guiding verse can help boys become more like Jesus mentally (smarter), physically (stronger), spiritually (deeper), and socially (cooler). From Bibles and devotionals to fiction and nonfiction, with plenty of gross and gory mixed in, there is something for every boy.

Bible Heroes & Bad Guys
Written by Rick Osborne, Marnie Wooding & Ed Strauss
Softcover • ISBN 0-310-70322-0

Big Bad Bible Giants
Written by Ed Strauss
Softcover • ISBN 0-310-70869-9

Available now at your local bookstore!

zonder**kidz**

Luke 2:52

As part of the 2:52 series for boys, these books will pique interest in the amazing creatures some of God's people saw and encountered, as recorded in the pages of Scripture. These books will excite, teach, and hold the attention of boys 8 to 12. Boys will come away from reading these books with knowledge of how to be deeper, cooler, stronger, and smarter for God.

Bible Wars and Weapons
Written by Rick Osborne,
Marnie Wooding & Ed Strauss
Softcover • ISBN 0-310-70323-9

Creepy Creatures &
Bizarre Beasts from the Bible
Written by Rick Osborne & Ed Strauss
Softcover • ISBN 0-310-70654-8

Weird & Gross Bible Stuff
Written by Rick Osborne, Quentin Guy
& Ed Strauss
Softcover • ISBN 0-310-70484-7

Available now at your local bookstore!

zonder**kidz**

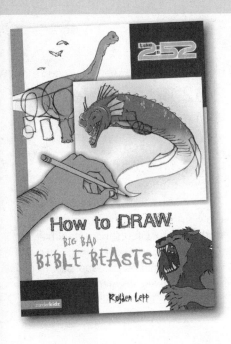

How to Draw
Big Bad Bible Beasts
Written by Royden Lepp
Softcover • ISBN 0-310-71336-6

How to Draw Big Bad Bible Beasts depicts both familiar and unfamiliar creatures from Bible times. It will help young artists visualize scenes from the Bible and use their creativity to reproduce them.

How to Draw Good,
Bad & Ugly Bible Guys
Written by Royden Lepp
Softcover • ISBN 0-310-71337-4

How to Draw Good, Bad, & Ugly Bible Guys depicts the dress and armor of people from Bible times. It will help young artists visualize scenes from the Bible and use their creativity to reproduce them.

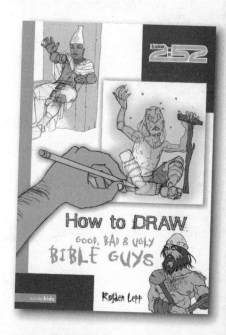

Available now at your local bookstore!

zonder**kidz**

2:52 Boys Bible
The "Ultimate Manual" for Boys
New International Version

Hardcover • ISBN 0-310-70320-4
Softcover • ISBN 0-310-70552-5

Finally, a Bible just for boys! Discover gross and gory Bible stuff. Find out interesting and humorous Bible facts. Apply the Bible to your own life through fun doodles, sketches, and quick responses. Learn how to become more like Jesus mentally, physically, spiritually, and socially.

NIV 2:52 Backpack Bible
Italian Duo-Tone™, Brown/Orange

ISBN 0-310-71417-6

The full NIV text in a handy size for boys on the go— for ages 8 and up.

Available at your local bookstore!

zonder**kidz**